OPTICIAN
TO THE STARS

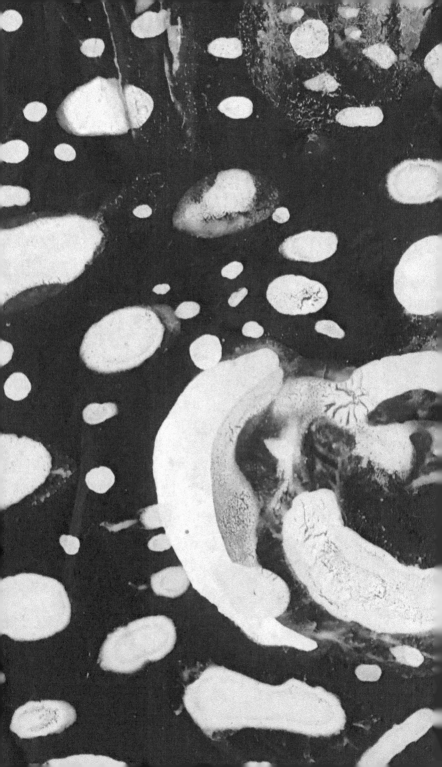

OPTICIAN TO THE STARS

New Poems

2022 — 2023

Todd Swift

◯◯◯ MAIDA VALE PUBLISHING

First published in 2024
by Maida Vale Publishing Ltd
Black Spring Press Group
United Kingdom

Typeset with artwork and graphic design by Edwin Smet

ISBN 978-1-915406-46-0

BLACKSPRINGPRESSGROUP.COM

IN MEMORY OF
MY FRIENDS, POETS

IAN FERRIER
KEVIN HIGGINS
NIALL MCDEVITT
ROBERT MARKLAND SMITH (SMITTY)
SAM EISENSTEIN
STEVEN HEIGHTON

GONE TOO SOON

ALSO, IN MEMORY OF
MY BELOVED FRIEND,
LETTY LEE DAHME
TEACHER, READER, LOVER OF HYDRA
WITH THE SOUL OF A POET

POET'S INTRODUCTION

I wrote most of these poems when 'a lot happened' – for everyone. While in the background (and sometimes forecourt) of a few of them, the death of the Queen, the collapse of one prime minister or another, and the Ukraine war, feature, there are also poems referencing the death of friends, and my slow recovery from being in hospital over Christmas 2021 with heart failure.

In March 2022 I was fitted with a CRT-D device – a defibrillator and pacemaker with three lines attached to the heart; and was on blood thinners for a blood clot in my heart, which remains as of date of this writing, although smaller. On 11 tablets a day for over two years, life is very different, but I have learned to manage as best as possible. I would like to record my gratitude here to the doctors, surgeon, nurses and others, who have helped me. These poems are not mainly narrative or descriptive of 'a time of illness' and are not presented in a strictly chronological fashion; this is not by any means a 'diary'.

These days, I publish a pamphlet or small book of poems annually, around Christmas or Easter; it is a way of somehow remaining true to my deep love of poems.

MAIDA VALE, LONDON, January 9, 2024

THE ICICLE

I cannot do what you can do
said the icicle to the match;
I cannot grow bigger with heat;
watch – in cold is my renewal;

yes said the little stick, but fuel
like mine depends on others
to be truly great – I am an agent
more than actor, critic not painter;

you gain your point by
slow degrees of thaw and freeze
to come to a deadly conclusion,
a dagger point of glinting sun;

in which I end, as if in your thrall:
yes he flared, but we coalesce
first at a dancing ball then lie
together on silver film, in a pool.

WHAT WINTER CAN DO

I know what winter can do.
It goes through and through
like a needle wants to sew.
It doesn't think it can ever thaw.

That is the weakness of ice
and snow. What they know
is themselves forever, which
is untrue. While they are

the everywhere of doing
they are thorough, like fire.
But winter is a formless liar
that disproves its logic twice;

once when a blizzard comes in
and when it withers away;
why it is so self-possessed
I cannot say, but so is summer.

AT LOWEST PEAK

at lowest peak
am still in mountains;
hard to complain
with a part to speak;
the ache under-shadows
like a valley is depression;
over weather in near snow
in circling air; one
thought repeats like music,
axe or be axed in this age;
such are ideas when sick;
words turn against the page.
Possibly rescue happens,
though not as often as lost.

TIRESOME THE WAY

we waste each other's time,
sadists with a miniature whip
cajoling nuisance and affray,
we dole out dismay
by being big-shots of disdain,
ladling the cold soup of pain,
the vicious viscose vichyssoise;
we could be gentler, but then
so could meteors, or a Kray;
the tendency is otherwise,
to say cutthroat things again
like when we first began piracy;
come on, release the grip, was
it so bad before all hate came
loose, the door-stringed canine
or incisor dangling its rosy line?

I AM NOT ONE OF YER ICONS OF POE

try apparently for reasons be
yond my own decisions like ex
istence or family but i persist o
kay? i have a soul to feed, a he
art that careers fitfully like pa
in, a weather system blasting a
way inside; name a day after t
his integral marbles spill or lo
se yer honest critical powers cu
z this work is a true fire frenz
y and denying elements is la
x diligence; i'm yer turmoil mad
e in spaced letters like a sign

NO ACCIDENT

things don't fall apart
they're dismantled or
let go from incautious
hands; thrown over,
knocked down, lobbed

like ignited bottles; art
is made – so is chaos
a most human skill,
the undoing of many
still to be born; heart,

mind, gut, spleen, all
have their part to play
in unravelling skeins,
recklessly pulled knots;
letting loose of caught

minotaurs or goddesses:
confess, it burns fraught
because we are: fire, flood,
famine, war, pooling out
as a stain does, evidentiary.

October 19, 2022

SCHOOLGIRLS OF IRAN

When we see
the schoolgirls of Iran
not playing but acting
as unafraid as any tree,
we know that poetry
is an idea whose time
comes in actions
not words alone; standing
up for a thing taller
than beauty, to be heard
and seen, to fan true
flames of history, to grow
a garden, an arbour, green
as every blade of grass,
to bring far fairness to pass.

POEM FOR NIALL MCDEVITT

You'd have it with cymbals,
jazz suit, with opiate Blake,
enjoy with underground kazoo,
tambourines, beat bodhran;
calm handsome cool, man!
Way too counter, bohemian,
to care what I might ever do
on your death; I'm shaken,
sickened, back to old school
here: no one in London knew
more about either great W.B. –
behind symbolic shades, saw
with visionary insight; all who
see true signs will mourn Niall.

MESSAGE SEND FAILURE

The chlorophyl doesn't reach
anymore; the fuel of trees
shorts out; fuses blown,
the strewn flares on
the leaf-red lawn
signal dying down –
embers of failed hours
glowing slowly to sleep,
the dream of bright summer
lighting poor wicks, bare
branches filled by frost;
not all is lost, but some are
taken in a trice; rustling
trick time of autumn mice.

HER MAJESTY

one thing holds another thing
like a round wedding ring.
or doesn't. the lynchpin,
spanning bridge strut
has a breakpoint. not so king
or queen. they outlast playing,
like ground's memory of rain.
continuing. on the drive
past, one coffin holds all
our shook feelings, more.
a sound reign is a building
that doesn't fall, foiled.
folds of the regal shroud
surging like thinking gold.

IN MEMORIAM

The storm has taken down
the tree, which stood
seventy seasons by four,
to leave the arbour restless,
without a roof's rising crown,
almost without a floor,
so skittering leaves flood
about, revealing lost acorns;
the forest is aghast, forlorn;
a tossed tempest grown out;
it is horrible emptiness.
There is a legacy that lasts
past loss, the quick torn apart –
roots only deepen to be flown.

September 8, 2022

ON CIRCUS ROAD I SAT DOWN,

in NW8, so I knew what I was doing
with a resonant trope,
circling the tightrope tighter,
after seeing my heart doctor,

not my heart's desire, no,
on the six month anniversary
of the cardiac implant for
a broken heart; we cope,

when we do, like Wendy,
taking cocoa; or like Yeats,
lamenting the circus animals
who got away. The young

actor from *Mad Max: Fury
Road* cycled past, a baby
strapped to his chest.
I was happy to see him ride.

I have eight years maybe,
or thereabouts, to keep on going.
To make a go of it all. Standing up
to endure feathered stallions

on a curving weathered saddle,
as if starring in the big show.
Or not. No point in acting up,
just to make a symbolic exit;

there's time left to write more,
if not better, and finally grow
adult enough to love-glide,
part barker, part swan, all heart.

LOVE MELTS, IS MOLTEN ORE.

I believe the flying
more than the bird;
the dying more
than the rising word;
truth is in the confusing
tumult of the lines above.

READING ABOUT DEATH

is the opposite of dying,
just as speaking
sets silence aside;
this is the spadework
language does for us,
placing the hole
that will become our
last place to one side
until it is filled by
whatever is our body
when the body says no
more talk of this, go, go.

NOT FOR THE FIRST TIME

have I brandished
my father's severed arm
at the Christmas table
waving it at my oblivious
mother and twenty
other various relations,
at the top of these lungs:
this is it, here it comes!
to relative silence,
well it is a silent night,
though in the constant dream
family and world violence
get muddied up; it's
happened before.

LIFE IS A HOLIDAY

it has to end: not ornate,
a simple sentiment
but true enough to say;
the deep sun burns,

the long sun inspires;
the romping sea turns
its eternal hidden wires;
the particular sand is hot,

the nights are arabesques;
writers in bed, lovers
at desks, send bold cards
about their sweet delays

in the gardens of an Alhambra;
after the seventh is the eighth;
we go into cold shade after
passing under the wine gate.

SPAIN

A slim young man rises
from the sea and stretches
out on the sand like a god

who is careless with things;
soon, his twin sister also
comes to lie down beside him;

or his lover; or curious doubling.
I can see them from where I lie
but I am not of their rank,

so I stay where I am, enjoying
the outside ring of the world,
that lets in the sunlight

even when we remain
in night-shadow.
The old sea never surprises.

TODD SWIFT

TOTAL ARTIFICIAL HEART

despite the textbook being
mostly 800 pages of science,
there is poetry in the cardiology

that's more than rhetorical,
but some of that leaks in too –
because naming and words

happen, and compensate,
like the total artificial heart
at the heart of the study,

your best 'next best thing
buddy', doing its beating
with style and aesthetic flare;

but is it real enough to care
or cure? That is art's ventricle asking, asking,
as only *always* may or can or does or will.

CAT'S PAW ON MY IPHONE

I could make a lot
from this.
Many images, wry
comments.
But I won't.
I simply won't make hay
or poetry
from a misplaced claw
or four
across a device
more harming than good;
there's no law or creature
to make me use every thing
in creation. Or being.

I SEE NOW

i gave my body not to
science but poetry
which did not need or
want said thing, but took

it greedily anyway
being a maw –
the hole seeping inwards
at the pit of our galaxy –

you pour out of yourself
into it, all your energy,
light, existing forms –
it whorling back,

crackling with indifferent
complexity, interior swarming
while you dissipate,
indeterminated.

ON READING LOUIS DUDEK

in retrospect not quaint,
failed or other critical complaint,

your work has a sturdy weight
like a made thing, its fate

to collect neglect like dust
only because all things must

in time turn from modern to old,
and from old to ancient, gold

light being the final aim
of all poetic craftspersons, fame

the accidental laurel some win,
most maker's lose, forgotten

in the sea of artful creation;
integrity the word I'd mention

as your earned label – hard-won
truth, your careful long devotion.

TODD SWIFT

EASTER IS

a dragon's egg:
the impossible
birthing the real,
something to
swallow that breaks,
soft interior,
but wings and fire
beat about
the exterior,
a frenzied world
of hectic
creatures, difficult
belief almost believed.

PRE-OP SPRING DAY IN MARCH 2022

It's been too long till spring –
   is false. It's here, in time.
just as it always was, a thing
   like a wheel or a poem, rhyme;

that is, it has its schedule,
   takes its turn, happens as it does.
Still, the sun climbing trees, I'm full
   to bursting with light's to and fros.

All is event, like thought, argument,
   war or love; like a pacemaker
device, implant I fear to have, spent
   hours returning like a general to their

tent. It's life itself that surveys
   maps, terrain, future battlefields.
Nothing less than this glorious day
   of impractical miracle-sun, big yields,

obliterates memories of lockdown, shelters
   underground, darkness that preys
on mind and heart-valves, those skelters
   that turn about like unlovers, May's

dancers around the burgeoning pole.
   I'm alive, for now, pre-op, thoughtful,
re-reading The School of Donne, again,
   to be reminded of a deceased friend

to look at a brilliant mind as a season
of circuitry, shock, and curative reason.

POEM DAY BEFORE MY 56TH BIRTHDAY

The perfect poem is out of sight, around the bend,
Part optic fibre cables being laid underground,
Part cherry blossoms staggeringly impermanent,
Outrageous as Stravinsky music in the air,

Part finely shattered, gold-re-joined, Satsuma vase,
Part so-brazenly broken national laws,
Part of the world as it moves around other worlds,
Part so personal it embarrasses even itself,

Part cruelly stern as a witchfinder general,
Part wonderfully iconoclastic as a witch's brew,
Part cat sleeping, part cat leaping, part paw,
Part mouse that got away; part all the pain

We ever knew, and then some, and then some more;
The treasure under the floorboards under the stairs,
Is being written for someone else's birthday,
By someone else; won't ever be written, to be true,

Because perfection is the enemy of any friend
To what is troubling to imagine, harder to rephrase.
That won't stop me from summoning this one up,
Stolen from the mystery shelf where language lies.

In my poem I'd need a bit of Canada, but not just snow,
Some parental turmoil and all that sorrow, saved
Somehow by compassion; sex of younger days, reviewed
By religion, marriage and sickness, the bumbling through.

Camaraderie bordering on true love, travel to odd climes;
The flats in Budapest, Paris and London, over-booked,
Overlooking trees; streets with prams not ever ours;
The hours, the hours, of forgiving and consoling powers.

April 7, 2022

SNOW

In Hampstead for Warfarin blood tests
I meet a lady with a cane at coffee after
who lives near Keats' house,
whose mother knew Louis MacNeice;

whose husband, post-pacemaker,
jumps from helicopters to ski;
and I recite to her the poem 'Snow'
about the sudden world, particular,

indivisible, and we speak of books,
how at Easter, she hides them
in her garden for her grandchildren,
like chocolate eggs; and then she leaves;

and I reflect on the world of strangers,
the world of blood, atomic, riven,
how this April the coldest winds are
being driven to us from Russian forces;

how the white snow looks like surrender
being torn up into a polyglot roar
of refusal, anger, and civilian defiance;
how I am thankful to the invisible maybe

of creation for more hours in this flurry
of experiences, talking, being vulnerable,
less dead than I could be, than others are,
as snow unseasonably becomes real.

April 1, 2022

THOUGHT

i don't think much
about what will never happen
except most of the time.

usually it involves playing
with two specially-carved bones
one in the shape of a heart

the other looking like a dagger.
risk is nearby, the rules say,
so is impossibly exciting danger.

it is a game of solitaire.
mostly i forget the name given
to the hour between love

and alpine-crisp despair.
but i never forget to roll a die
and its twin like a pair

of vultures was paying me
a visit out of doubtful duty.

DEATH REVISITED

when you are gone
you will not miss any thing
but if you could
it would be
rain

THEY WEAR SHADES

For Steven Heighton

I was the optician to the stars
in a time of occluded skies,
polishing the convex concavities

with something akin to flair, if not ease,
surgically fitting lens into frame,
as if vision was sight not a separate thing

acting on the seen – anyway visuality
is always flawed, bent so far as if a steel
bar under strain – magnification tends

to pain some corneal affairs: squinting
at the sun the par excellence of that flaw
in the optical glass.

DEATH OF HIGGINS 1

in time i will get over your death
because i will be dead too.
some people try to liven things
up with recreations of ABBA
winning something or other
on a transistor radio borrowed
from a homeless ex-priest
who now thinks Dawkins is God
and considers urine ambrosial;
but basically a corpse is a blank
slate on which writing anything
is not borderline criminal, but
actually borderline and criminal;
pills only slow death; as you
can observe within a hundred
or less years; then goodbye
smart phone, hello dumb skull.

DEATH OF HIGGINS 2

at times like this
I'd prefer another time.
like the one where the big fat
cheque for the little thin poem
was handed over pronto
during the sort of applause
they bottle and sell in North
Korea, to a variety of cretins;
no, not now, I am busy basking
in not being you; or me.
but this is the big one –
being a being's tough punch –
oblivion's plus size pantaloons;
the big lunch bill unasked for
brought on a faux silver tray
by the barely apologetic goon.

TODD SWIFT

SMITTY, RIP

It's become the time that isn't poetry –
a loss list instead of
the permanently dead.
Catholic, us, yet I find
your absence not a case for rejoicing
at heaven's gain –
just the ordinary
sadness death of friends begins
to be at my age. Never ends, these
moments when we get an email and
then someone's gone.
I could try and strum
a rhyme out of you to retail,
maybe later. Today I'm numb.

THE WISE

Every Christmas is a Christmas:
all the first things happen,
and the last – those flutters that
seem centuries apprehensive
for Santa; hearing hoofs at night
wanting snow; getting less;

the drink, shouts, tears – or
Jovial unbolting calm all day,
as if love was no longer aloof;
and the lying in hospital, paper
hat askew on the almost-skull;
presented with bearable turkey

like a cracker's finite humour;
the more and less of the birth
is how it unifies lonely and loved
in one unlockable story, so open
we are all implicated, on earth;
time jolts back to find pain light.

I would have thought to have
had it done by now, this gift
being made by the way of me
moving through the world,
spindrift that I am, as if we gave

not of ourselves, but actually
ourselves, which we do, artist
whose fist comes uncurled,
who makes as if casually, by
just doing what happens to be

done; from run of the mill
to sometimes extraordinary –
but it has been delayed now
by a snow event unfolding
like maddened paper; slow

delivery this present, absent
after all; so I will instead provide
like the drummer boy all hours
when my heart pounds not yet
having died, or skipped its work.

CRUCIFIXUM DOCET VERITATEM

I am there now, the place where I can say to you directly What the tricks of language Can hinder or form, I know that to keep it interesting Is the price of attention, you go Variously across the field, It's a show, and a tell, but the main fact Is talking, some sharing, a gesture Out to another, maybe a friend Who is not even real, yet, An apparition of apprehension, Expected attendee at the imaginary Reading in the heaven of elsewhere, That place without pornography, Alcohol, violence, pills, and screaming; That ice palace of peace, unlike any Genuine mind, I am on the boil, A lobster reddening, on ferocious Pain attention, it's all apart now, Not yours, not mine, just a body with soul Tied to it, as they say in poems; I am the messenger, do not spare me; Show the crowds your un-empathy; It's strong to be empty and immediate, I am pierced daily by Memory and experience; epistemology Proves that the facts are solid, and sharp; Lie on the gurney and leak Into the bucket like a butchered animal Grateful for love; I am the message and I come to say You've been petty; You're scared, but cut it out, we see through The fear, the protecting ranking of the sickly canon; You kill the art that you feed on; Go home and consider your positions. My sheet lightning will light the way.

STATEMENT FROM THE PRESIDENT OF IRELAND

No more poet deaths
will be allowed until we can all
catch our breaths, make it down
to the local bookshop even if
boarded up or turned online
retailer due to the Covid, and buy
copies of the departed,
who laboured so long
at the uncomprehending wall
of your insensitive ear drums,
you thick lacklustre eejits
who never met a poetic line
you didn't prefer to end, whose love
of enjambment is a misreading of what jam is.

THE YEAR 2022

Hard hating a year
that kept you somehow
alive – even at a cost;
each past new eve
ends up lost. But we keep
re-inventing the confetti
wheel; dance little bubbles
dance! Some people are
paid to sweep away glitter,
sleep in the past, awake
in the moment to fear;
happy happy! Poss-
ibly should be, more. Thanks!
Trouble is, time unspools too.

GIFT

Inside the green box
was a typed note
that said
I wrapped this in
after I was dead;
there was nothing
else, no socks
or coat; no red ring.
On the other side
of the bond paper:
I was born later.

VERIFIED ARTIST

he'd sit and time the orchestra
then turn and say: a minute fast
he was funny that way; artist
of the stopwatch, a fan of sorts
he verified chronology for fun,
or another synchronous reason,
wanting a part to play in music
otherwise only distantly seen;
and here's the turn to that,
the Volta in my pocket,
I met him once and moved on
but kept the image for a poem,
like leaving a door unlatched
so later someone could come in.

GRIM ISLAND

mostly uninhabitable
for human kind /
don't come here
even say
the local cannibals :
we are unwelcoming
to your kith and kin
plus our weather /
is a double sin
sun a nasty rumour
so stay away !

i realise that what i do
everyone does
and isn't amazing: poetry
is just breathing words,
living across a page;
i am no one anymore,
feel boring as a lost cause;
billionaires plus influencers
are important, will last;
my purpose is a past,
when skill, art & care
were valued, & reading
deep, well, intensely aware;
only surface beauty is real,
as well as power & money.

i'm sad again always
it is the bluest day does
the dud work of digging
a maze under my brain
dragging my heels nowhere
into a slow sulking lane
because life is tougher
than nails in the arm bones
my friends – you listeners
lost somewhere on the way
from ten to fifties – Jeezus
how the small fall like petals
not put together again
turmoil somehow pent in
so better try better hopings

i don't have any real money,

got precious little fame,

played a minus zero sum game –

so send me the Easter Bunny,

and all burnt Easter Island too,

to top denuded baskets up,

with plovers' eggs, break a few,

for my cracked breakfast cup,

am tired of hearing about light

in stuff, about prizes even more,

there's already day and night

in living, shut oversized doors;

wish i'd been paid in new honey,

could heal the plenty maimed.

shaping the shapeless past,

peeling the first grape last,

assuming the azimuth

to pyramid owlish truth –

roll in a growling surf,

wildly toss your dandy scarf,

the delirious curfew is tolling,

bell towers blown apart by drones,

harsh thunder rolling,

meteoric rhetoric dramatic

with a Masonic Boom Mozart owned –

art throws war aside like skin,

parts seas, amid crushing looms,

wine rises.

i didn't win and nor did you
the golden guy or rose tattoo,
encrusted falcon or crystal shoe
but then again we hardly tried;

sure we flew on the big red eye,
wore a long gown, tied a bow,
doctored it down, killed off a bit
for sold darlings when we pried

trust out; gamed for a screen
what was rarely seen, but honey
knew from a start it was the lie;
it's tinsel and Gretel, light heavy

metal, old Cagney's mad shout –
nope never had that kinda clout,
names left outside the envelope.

when i was toddling young
death didn't exist
which is a big gift that
kept getting taken away
not every day but often enough;
rarely wept or slept rough;
it was a brief stay of execution
you might say; a false dawn,
or even a thrifty heaven, one
without much intake of stuff,
fake as glass diamonds cutting
little ice; it was a lie, bitterly
nice, the opposite of life, cool
artifice like Oscar Wilde; it
died and ended me as a child.

i am going to start my poem
as if this was the commencing of the very universe itself so
imagine the first i on line one as the place just after that infinite
loneliness known as the pre-bang or otherwise anti-being, minus
zero, now keep going back to that opening action of deciding to
begin with i not light or you or God or some spell or inducing
arcana, some word or The Word; no, i instead, self placed after
nothing, thus, proclaiming my origin to be valuable. becoming is
the world.

weird wallpaper, books –
they move
about, like no tomorrow
ever does –
out of the paper, off
the wall – the shelf
all of it, in undulant
action, a style in form –
so that the very place
becomes a tome –
the longest, deepest
ever – forest of what ifs –
jimmied floor to roof –
canopy copying life itself

freewheeling doesn't cut it
don't think this is free
it costs energy of mind
at least plus body plus maybe
soul to craft this spill, form
the mess of intelligence into
art or some appearance of art;
it may seem informal to you,
but to me it's internal combustion
with the horses escaping the barn like furies;
Muses are not our dance friends always
they demand returns; the bridle enhances
as it restrains, the rush gets real.

someone i love has died
or someone else, or some body
i barely know, but may be close
to you – someone is dying, as we
always knew, but often try
to avoid; we don't appreciate
a looming void; and who is the we poems address?
also an emptiness akin to God,
or any concept you care to provide;
someone i love is gone or going
to a better place, or none; stoics die
as often as nervous criers;
it is either sad or ok or whatever you decide
to feel; we are a meal for
mystery; disappearance;
even resurrection. someone is love.

i keep writing poems
what else can i do?
the sun is going soon,
i have yet to break through
to the place of true wonder
where every word's a lustre
every gesture looks true,
the carnival of mirrors
where i can dance with you;
all the endurable fears,
the sly hours of composition,
none of it adds up to a comb
from your nightstand, tears
from a sea glass eye; love
made me make these tombs
where none of me will lie.

i gave you the weapons,
i sang you the right songs,
i dressed your drummer boys,
i recalculated your wrongs.
i underfunded your joys,
i underwrote your squalor,
i oversaw your parade grounds
i overlaid your deathly pallor.
now you don't want to pay,
which is a big category error;
refusing tax means one thing:
death unrolls its easy terror.
governing isn't for the weak,
be strong, say what you speak.

i am drawn to the darkness
like a moth to an unlit flame;
Jesus loves me this i know
but there is a beast still to tame;
Annunciation arrives with light
in tow; a good time to be had
by all, jeering at the crucifixion
which failed let me remind you:
the ultimate criminal escaped,
he died, spent hours in the bad,
then stood to rescue us all – action hero
for the ages; learn to turn
those bible pages. burn
for better yearnings if you can.

TODD SWIFT

most of my poems were self-
fixated, but alter that to are,
too often the vehicle was ego
egged on to drive a wordy car;
not much heft in monomania,
beyond the thriller stacks,
but i was the Lizzie Borden of
narcissistic regard, and gave
my own autofocus endless whacks –
because, i guess love found an echo
in my reflection, to mix the spectre
with the feast; i put own desires first
foremost and others much more least;
espoused Christ as if easiest to care for Thou,
not me; have messed my hair and soul,
to appear inspired; but it is time to retire
vanity and do more with rhyme than show, possess.

if we had some time together,
if we found ourselves alone,
we might reinvent hot weather,
rip out every wire or phone,
tape up every screen, close
all the windows, open books
to lay on the pillows, while we'd
pretend worship on the floor;
there'd be splinters by the end,
flour and dust in the air, petals
thrown about like loose talk,
flowers in the bathtubs, well,
the stems and stalks; stockings,
socks, knee-highs, Lederhosen
hung from chandeliers, corks
strewn like lies from a podium;
obliterate dying's tedium.

TODD SWIFT

GOOD FRIDAY

The day I was born, '66 –
a route that another Todd took
on television, my mother's
favourite show that year;
surprising I was not called Jesus

given the auspicious day instead;
or Nicodemus or Paul.
Now please kneel. Now stand.
Was it planned? Not me, look
I meant the betrayal among

crushed olives. Christ fell
into Saturday's calumny,
converting the lives lost there.
Yes it was intentional, hell,
the vinegar, spear, tomb, tears.
Sin requires a lot of road to fix.

it is always someone's birthday
but today is mine!
because i am spoiled and selfish
or want to be the world itself
for awhile; and why not?
i fought in my incubator
for the right to this day's ego;
death will put me in my place;
in the meantime, let all born
on this April slice of calendar
riot to proclaim their being here,
their spring joys and fears,
being universally important if
only in their own ageing minds.

a glass of water
like a crying monocle.

a bowl of sugar packets
like a divided electorate.

a can of knives and forks
like an invention yet to occur.

a self-published paperback
like all the babies in the world.

this is what reality looks
like when poetry's king.

a young poet thinks
everything is important.

an old poet knows
nothing is that important.

a young poet
falls in love daily.

an old poet feels
dying more each year.

a young poet grows
into an old poet, not always.

bah! I am tired of being ignored,
Glaucus, as a poet by fools –
those not gods, like your sea self
see, deeper into immortality,
I make words swim like dolphins!
What shall I do to survive
without a raft of fame to cling to
in the waves of cold misfortune?
Barely read, I remain beached
too often, when my cetaceans
should soar like winged fish!
You are glittering like inspiration
and know the cost of greatness
requires foregoing mere human
passions – an artist by leap!
Can you stir a storm to drown
the sleeping world, awaken
a creature wise enough to love
my begotten things? I sink
in thoughts, want to be known,
not for my own sake but singing.

We are not meant to say
exactly what we think
in poems, but come sideways
to the brink
of the matter, but to hell
with such delay:
a bullet tore the throat out
of Sudan's great singer
as she walked for food
near her home in a war
only a damn fool would fight;
no – worse, an evil fool
wanting power instead of song;
it kills music, kills light, kills good.
I say it here without skill:
war is pure wrong dumb shit.

The day I lost my poetic edge
pulled magnets off the fridge,
knowing words way past due,
beauty smelling off, truths few,
but kept a sense of gentle elan,
as if lyrically bereft was a plan,
went out to smell roasted coffee,
rest on the gate to ogle trees,
felt distant fatality in the wind,
knew myself to be mostly kind,
gave up all dreams of literature,
moving on to pastures mature,
a growing older without the pain
of forever questing for a refrain.

CORONATION DAY

Uninvited and alone,
the gas meter fitted
with a lock owned
by billionaires, she puts on
the telly to see a rainy London
put on its airs and folly;
she's read *Vanity Fair*,
went to uni, when it was free,
knows history by its dates
and wars, the endless
obituaries of fate; she pours
herself an early one, Pimm's,
stands to toast her and him,
not so much as Queen or King
but as the cost of living here,
so close to power or oblivion.

keep writing!
the critics know little
and we are all dead soon;
keep writing!
it hurts no one, very much,
and may give some pleasure
one day; and even if
you are totally forgotten
and never read, well,
that's only what every bird
experiences,
or
flower or spring! The flowing
without recognition of nature
is also alive, beautiful, true!

new april books
from the paris bookshop
avril 2023
that fresh smell,
the little red wrappers
with those prizes,
poetry, philosophy, feminism,
in a language i sort of read
84 euros for 6 books plus
a pamphlet!
heaven on earth!
walking out with the paper
bag, to sit in the sun
even with all the evil going on
there is subtle hope in these

The Paris that we loved
has moved

The one now is even better
and less fettered

Other cities claim to be
what Paris is

The world in all its glory
and its mess

Great Snowstorms
of the Past
and Future
is the name of my next
book of poems
maybe
or just a passing idea
like a blizzard
becomes a flurry
in time

Marcus A. tells me I already
know what it is to be dead,
having not been, before
when I was not yet conceived –
it is only like that, he consoles;
ah, not true Caesar Aurelius
I say – for now I have tasted
cherries, seen cherry blossoms
in the wind, heard voices
singing, read wild poetry;
to go now is to leave behind
things once known, a party
of friends in the other room,
my having to go to bed
forever like a punished child.
Having existed then not
is a great relinquishing.

I publish mainly on Instagram
these days
as you know, my friends –
not in the golden books,
prized pages of the emperors
of glancing fame and power;
now is not my hour
of chance acclaim; I am a cat
in shadows or a lost fox,
moving as best befits outcasts;
I keep to my own channels,
know the yards I may freely
visit. Do not pity me.
You who glimpse my poems
have shared a private dance
in the midnight of visitation.

i'm not in this body
much longer
i better get my soul
built stronger
or whatever will be
looking down
at me
when the priest
and doctor say
final orders
but least of all
i should pay the bills
since money isn't
coming any further
than death's four walls

You know the truth as well as I –
there is no more truth in a prize
for poetry than a lie; it's not
archery, is it? The measure's
not a bullseye. It's entirely sized
up by how and why the reader
thinks and feels already; plus
a bit of open mind if they try.

no one owns poetry
though many try;
a mistake of taking,
a doing by making
which breaks no law
but one: hubris, or, why
kiss a sleeping stone
to create a princess?
magic is a metaphor,
like a simile is a lie
dressed as a manticore;
as if no necromancer
knows more than a rhymer –
one raises the dead, the other
builds grave markers
that survive when all have gone.

one day I was ancient;
my columns half gone, jagged
style, like in that song by
Siouxsie – in dust, shambling
along, my pinstripes sideways,
everything awry but not
in an ironic, knowing way –
it was the dawn of an age
where I felt age; but a-historic,
not written about by Hesiod
or Gibbons, Apollonaire;
my postmodernity was blown,
my identity shown to be olden;
the wind made my pink tie raise
itself like an empty gesture.
I felt older than pyramids.

FYI

i have been drinking
which is none of your business
but i am temporarily
at one with all things
however family members may
have been drunks
and my meds interact
with booze, so
this splendour is doomed;
must end, like the universe;
many critics recoil from
expressions of real feelings;
as if distance was more than
a foil for empire, conquest;
irony is a choice, so is direct
treatment; i am writing
under an influence, deal.

i have known a hard truth
you can have also,
i will gift it to you, it is sore,
it is not easy to know,
still, it keeps the self sharp
as a scythe in the grass
to go forward keen
with strong knowing,
the mind keeps busy mowing,
needs to clear the way
ahead; it is this, here:
the best diamonds are in webs,
dew caught by sun, soon gone;
the world values the wrong
ones most often; you deserved
more, but the light saw you truly.

had this to be the final note
the first to go is rhyme –
no time for that fuss; but
i'd miss it still, the shaping
will is beautiful as it floats
across lines on a surface;
next to sacrifice, metaphor
and its kin; poems speak,
they don't have to perform
for their supper; at its peak
a mountain is its meaning,
you don't climb further;
Alvarez was a climber, elite,
he knew much, taught
to be smart if passionate;
leave just a raw soul forming
a mind in words to be shared,
be good, bare, my love, my all.

i know the other styles
i know what they can do
this poem travels miles
built for the more not few
we could be innovative
or opt back to old lore
let's tack to basic creative
and aim for the heart's core;
words like to rhyme in couplets
though other ways are cool;
the language wears doublets
and still capers like a fool;
there's not much left to say:
we die, so love, go live this day.

ON NOT BEING A KING

Less rich, less majestic,
less entitled, less ensconced,
less embattled, less potent,
less landed, less connected,
less constrained, less noble,
less invested, less powerful,
less divine, less right,
less followed, less unamused,
less betrayed, less questioned,
less busy, less leisured,
less driven, less fed,
less travelled, less housed,
less fearful, less guarded,
less wise, less informed,
less costumed, less loved,
less coined, less cheered,
less favoured, less beheaded.

writing in the dark
don't worry about me
there's the phone's star
predetermining my wise
journey to a child god here;

or would it were so,
but along the sleepless way
comes Cheap Trick 1977
via Spotify's cold omniscience
coming over like a knowing

friend or maybe lover;
it's only night; it ends;
a search makes its own finds,
writing is where
the manger lies.

you may have a small jaw
or no jaw at all
but keep smiling, baby
the sun is bigger than law

you may be short at the bank
or bank's gone broke
but keep dancing, love
moon rose up when sun sank

you may be pretty as Jesus
or pretty crucified
but keep walking, dear
night and day will guide us.

There comes a time
and bright, it has
passed and then some,
games of footfall, fine
fettle, youth's broken tomb,
all is honeycombed loose,
a dazzling misadventure
of sun, itself the prime
flight; the old numbers come
back, if ever even gone,
as songs return each season
with new feathers, plumage
of pillaging firebirds, setting
alight plumed horizons.

there is no answer
to the mysteries.
the world flows on,
as if to say river, river
forever; it is a serious
stillness in the centre,
the long grass motionless
only the silence moving,
saying river, river;
and it scares even itself
here. this is where we die,
in a quiet meeting place
where water and dryness are
one touch of face or hand.

have i forgotten
what it was
when young
that kept me on
that single path
through my grandfather's
forest, his few good acres
of woodland, down
to the pond,
the size of a coin,
cool muck, skimmed by
the infinitesimal creatures
that thrive unrecorded
usually, in history? yes,
i no longer feel the awful
slime on my feet, dark
lid of chilling water, upsurge
into glade light, to dry
in youth's wasteful sun;
how being alone then
was terrifying, pure isolation,
the universe on all sides pressing,
the rest of things nowhere near,
this pinpoint moment's surety fixed forever,
my thin pale body somehow there,
constantly feeling itself.

drinking alone
with my phone
bittersweet symphony
on the pub radio
singing to me
as if i didn't know
how roller derby living
can be; i could connect
maybe to some other soul
but for now the peroni
keeps me company
and the bad news,
the weather of all things
that is always at our elbow.

it has become increasingly
the world
at the windows like a wind,
battering to high heaven
any sense of sense – whirlwind
agog amok in a whorl –
no time for respite, batten
down the sails, tie your body
to the thing that slips
forward on the big storm –
move with the whirligig, sailors!
all that is happening is
the time like ice
cracking knuckles at the pole,
sun like a wicked eye blazing.

forgive
forgive relentlessly –
rage is a drink too far
in the heart's bordello –

bite anger's pillow,
swallow the need
to hunt them down
one by one, with skills

honed by years of hate;
relent
relent religiously,
throw your revenge

to the four winds; be
ludicrously kind – surprise
everyone with your mercy;
taste gentleness on the air

like the first hint of spring.

ROSE POETRY

There is a rose
in every poem,
there are roses
all through this one:

words are a garden
my rose love;
and thorns besides;
no one goes through

roses without being
touched by first petals
then the other sting:
love is all at once

injury then pardon,
being carried to the tower
to live or die, as a flower
does, which is or is not cut.

In the heat hit garden
shade makes an island
around my chair,
and on it are three books:
Gide being immoral,
Archer too gentle to kill,
and one to edit for work;
the water beyond is sunlight,
the inverted metaphor
turning the river dry-bright;
I could live on my sudden eyot,
the river round is fresh,
I would keep an eye out for fish,
brute summer turns my mind
to fleshly things, or paper,
content to float between
the written and heating worlds,
one ruining the other fallen,
both in this instant a new Eden.

POETRY

Other things have more weight,
like the Sistine Chapel, a pail
filled with Miami Beach,

a Titanic-sized replica of the Titanic –
some have more height as in the Moon,
or an Olympic high jump in slow motion,

a hand from God or the Moon times two;
but nothing else is a poem once a poem
gets good and going.

pour soul, poor soul,
you are rich in words,
poems never hurt you
just poetry as a toil;
don't spoil your world
with critical worry –
do, spirit, go forth
your worth is never
going to increase
with a nod from
some committee
did a bee ever win a prize?
dolphins laugh at awards;
put the sword of want down
soul you are already
more than they say ever
listen to the moon, the air,
i like going on having left
the need for accolades behind
no one can stop a poet
who no longer fears a judge.

WINTER SOLSTICE

Light and dark
Embark

On a walk together
In the park

For more than fun –
They both have work

To do, with the sun.
The light goes first –

Then it is done –
The dark is alone.

This won't go on
For very long –

Soon, the light
Will be longer than

The dark's full span.
They share the world

And actually get along
Just fine, so long as

Both respect boundaries,
Don't cross key lines.

Both belong, contain part
Of what the other denies.

This is a poem
for Instagram
Not too long
and full of feeling
Love is good
Mean is bad
Red is blood
lowercase is sad.
Punctuation
sometimes if at all.
Small is wisdom.
Burn the candle
at both. Ends

I struggle daily
not to pack it in;
a few things save me
not precisely things
first, to quit this maelstrom
is a sin; second, my partner
and my family; third, friends,
fourth, the device on my heart
paid to provide a certain rhythm;
fifth, the daring small blood-clot
sized like an apple-core
waiting like a sleeping spy
on the wall of my right ventricle
jeering me on to die
then last, sixth, a stubborn part
that says don't let them win;
though the them is vague
could even be
cold days or bills;
so I take the medical tablets
or as we say in Canada, the pills.

I think in words, I think,
or words think me,
as has been argued
in words, something eludes

me today, though I see roses
or their name, dwindling at
the end of September
like full stops becoming ellipses.

By this I mean language has stepped in
to the picture, and tried to make
a new friend out of an experience,
risky game but it sometimes works.

It is enough to be in the world
without the fence of words
getting in the way... but an
open field is a space to play

sometimes lose one's way.
Myocardial flowers appear
like swords bent back in flame.

He says on his podcast death
never happens in the mind
when the mind ends then;
so it never happens to you.
To who, then? Not another,
or no one? To a friend?
The body is not the issue;
it is the mind. So he says.
He is not someone who prays,
which is okay. Which is fine;
he's a popular atheist online.

That's a career, is a way to earn.
You can learn even from devils;
and maybe he is being factual.
There may be no Hell or Heaven.
You exist then don't. No soul
or spirit or resurrection or
transmigration at all. Total zero.
Which is well, which is terrifying.
Which is why we think a future
after dying. Can't blame trying
even if the thought's impossible.

There have been other moments
but this is the one tonight,
cat's chin on my calf,
conked out in entirety

then my partner scuttled
on my right thigh, down
in sleep's deep sea chasms,
and it being a warm September

this is more than pleasant,
this is how to die,
with my two ultimate friends
reliant upon my body's stiller

qualities to stay in Nod's ride;
but that's lyrical beauty talk,
cruelly disproved by Libyan
floods, Moroccan quakes;

the time it takes to sing
can also bring disasters to kill;
life is what death also makes.

Wallace Stevens was reading
his King James bible when
he wrote of the nothing
that is and the nothing
that is not there – Luke 8:17 –
for there is nothing hidden
that will not manifest, nothing
concealed that will not come
into the light; his mind of snow
knew the slight difference
between a quote and revision;
how to make a poem from
verse and chapter ex nihilo,
for creation springs from winter.

TODD SWIFT

My poems may not be yours,
they shape by their own style,
you don't have to fly on floors
to go that extra leg or mile;
of course there will be fashions,
parameters to apply like laws,
art critics risk defying passions
sternly ruling against all flaws;
I like these peccadilloes, errors,
grandiloquent conversations
with smart penguin emperors;
let performance be its occasion,
forms play above their station.
The kingdom's an agape door.

I don't have to put on airs
or wear bells on my shirts,
or caper like a character,
to prove to councils or the law

that I profess poetry a bit
when not partaking of the dirt
of human winter and its thaw;
I sing, shout, exclaim, utter,

bandy, exaggerate in rhyme,
in rickety flow, to try to climb
the mountain where goats are,
who, remember, spend time

with their own bedfellows,
to parastate. I'm confidently
real to self-creating aims,
grand or slightly small as they

stand to be described. Resist
situations of determination,
break out of every anticline.
I revel in being what I best do.

Autumn begins in sun
this time like a trick
the world is doing
with rotation, pulling light
out of season, but
most of us suspect soon
night will arrive with a moon
asking to see our tickets;
meaning, someone has to pay
for surprising illumination,
and today is brilliant play,
the gold on the lips that lies,
because to kiss poison
thinking it is beauty is to die.

rain shoves
October through
the slot for bills
as if weather wasn't bad
enough without the chill
in my mind, selfish as life,
telling me to hide forever,
to curl like a ball until
everything in the past
and present turns the channel
from human war to birds or seals;
nature feels less cruel than us;
it hurts even being real.

nothing, and then a flood
of fire as a noise, shedding blood;
a swan taking out the sky with wings
of flame; the air stabbed in the eyes,

a pounding of dying in name and act,
as the world shreds itself
for victory's gain; a word turning
on a spit above an inferno

that was a brain; it is thought
but physical, there; the kill-zone
has arrived, a god in shape and power,
burning all seen, felt, heard, skin,

hair; hate fills the clouds, then rains;
pity invisible, innocence blamed.

language has stopped working.
did it ever do?
too much is happening.
make it stop.
what you call reality is
what i call else.
put the souls back in. drop
please the horror-pit. we,

meaning all, need it. meaning
else. the else of less this. no.
no show can do more. pause.
law stopped. no boundaries
in fear. ask it for a good answer.
hate history. history harm.
berserk. birds strike. too much.
this could say names. places hit.

the point is never that. redirect.
around this edge is nightmare.
over that horizon. into worse.
there is horror on top of words
moving also under like worms.
don't make art try. it breaks
at a certain point. pointing out
this time. how this now occurs.

Fittingly if not according
to plan, the silence
at the Cenotaph, on TV,
is broken across two minutes
by a baby someone has
in their arms in the crowd;
veterans and everyone else
shift uneasily, aware this
isn't silence as they know it;
in the eye of commemoration
a storm of newborn life,
calling out miserably,
standing in for the war dying
unable to be heard under fire.

November, dark already
was it ever light?
Night flight, the world
is taking, night flight.
I put a film on,
set the dark TV bright,
about a war, a tight
spot they're in.
Fighting, some dead,
Lindy-hopping, ends
all right. Day is hours now
on the other side. Somehow
we must cross sleep's ferry,
wake when it's again bright.

BLACK CAT ON A GARDEN TABLE

It happens once
then again, then constantly –
seen to shaped to received –
the law of light, of poetry –
it cannot matter what is said
of a work of art
if listening to the work saying
already the everything it is,
which is both exaggeration
and religious truth;
the moment the black cat
rushes into the garden
there is a cat and garden
for as long as existence moves
into the more that is also beauty.

FAST POEM FOR IAN FERRIER

Yes, this is the fast poem,
Because it's from Todd Swift,
And who hasn't heard that one before?
Self-centring aside, this is actually for

Ian Ferrier, that ambling, shambling
Bear of a man, the great, enigmatic heart
Of Montreal spoken word,
Whose hoarse rasp, whose growl,

Whose shifting tones, maybe a howl,
Made him central, for allophone,
Francophone, anglophone, down the phone –
In getting it done, getting it said;

He recorded, he inscribed, he replayed,
He broadcast – throwing his presence
Wide, but carrying so many other voices
In his capacious sidecars. He made

CDs into books, books into CDs,
Was always there, the mystery guy,
Huge, but shy, who gruff and gentle
Took the mic to emcee, to invite –

To turn cold Quebec nights into poetry.
No one had more integrity, more time
For making it work for others, for sharing
Talent and vision. He provided bearings

When there was no map for these ways
Of doing something with words barely
Seen or heard before. He was a gathering.
Safe home, be well, go where it always speaks,

Makes noise, is listening, is said.
I won't make the next rhyme, will delay.
I thank you Ian, and love you, and am glad
You were there, in the milieu you mainly made.

October 2, 2023

PERSON OF THE YEAR, TAYLOR SWIFT

I'm someone else
With the same initials,
My own life exploding into greatness
On a distant screen but everywhere.

Not pain or sadness, really, just loss –
As if my twin sister had been
Stolen from me when we were nine,
Now found again in a big house

Strangely nearby – but unable
To recall us at all, anymore.
My life turns out to be about
Not being her, the un-Taylor,

Instead, get to be the trivia
Answer to the question: identify
The other T. Swift who wrote things
Down, in 2023. My love calls me Swifty.

COST-OF-LIVING CHRISTMAS, 2023

Her dreams are all the bare shelves
Stocked by swivel-eyed post-Covid elves –

They won't deliver the gifts the children ask for,
As if making a list or checking it twice mattered;

No, the truth is, this Christmas the tree'll
Stay dark; bills in flurries, unready meals...

And she prays for an election in the new year.
Santa helps those who help themselves.

COVENTRY CAROL

I am at Coventry in this carol now.
It is on my Wonderboom.
Sing like a dirge becoming birth –
Reverent beyond reverence –
As befits a mighty child so small
But crammed with God
To the maximum. I am heartsick,
But know Jesus does not approve attacks
Like when the bombers came across
The sky, led by a starlit night,
To lay Coventry low as any lamb.
I kneel to pray because of love,
Sick of the world, for what it does.
My heart gutters, like fat wax.
There is a wick in the blood for fire.

Bring your greatcoat
And lipstick, friend,
Bring your enigma machine
And stockings, ally,
Let's watch the frost settle
On failing high streets –
The Sunak-era is so cold –
Bring your silk parachute
And French chocolates, dear,
Fetch your victory gin,
Apocalyptic verse, and
Surreal love notes, we
Need them all now there's
A war on – the snow fits us
Like an airman's left glove –
Flying over this miserable kingdom.

SADNESS IS DESPAIR FOR BEGINNERS

No, not fair, sadness is December –
It has its cold moments of glitter,
Hope's gift rays, it comes and goes,
Despair stays – hunkered down
Like a guest from the side of the family
You'd prefer to disown – both those
Horses have thrown me down –
Cold days of little light
Let them out of their stables
To take me on – but they do let me ride –
Carrying me along, farther
Than one might expect to go –
For they bear so much,
Have their dreadful dull uses.

POET'S BIOGRAPHY

Todd Swift is a British-Canadian citizen, was born Good Friday 1966 in Montreal, Quebec and is one of the leading Canadian poet-anthologists of his generation.

He has a PhD from UEA. He once came third in the election for Oxford Professor of Poetry. He was poet in residence for a year at Pembroke College, Cambridge. He has organised reading events in Hungary, France, Canada, the USA and the UK. He was Oxfam poet in residence for ten years, and has edited and created dozens of anthologies and poetry DVDs and CDs.

Professor Mark Ford has called him 'The Orson Welles of Contemporary Poetry'.

A Catholic convert, he is married to an Irish barrister-solicitor; and is a godfather to Alex. A debating champion throughout his school, college and university years in Canada, he was a child prodigy who wrote his first novella by the age of three.

He has written over 100 hours for Fox, Disney, HBO, Paramount and the CBC, and was story editor for anime classic *Sailor Moon*. He is included in three of the key Canadian anthologies of his era, and co-edited the fourth for Carcanet. He lives in London, and loves cats.

His own poetry collections number over a dozen now.

PAST PRAISE FOR EARLIER COLLECTIONS

'[...] a dapper sense of style' – Emily Berry

'[...] uncommon panache and intelligence' – Srikanth Reddy

'A voice for our time' – Derek Mahon

'His voice is powerfully his own, but poetry lovers will find the grace notes of plainsong TS Eliot, but also the verbal dexterity of Robert Bringhurst' – George Elliott Clarke

'Sincerity and comedy attuned to a subtle ear' – Daljit Nagra

'Some of his lyric moments are joyously Audenesque'
– Fiona Sampson

'Swift has a beautiful sense of the rhythm of the English language' – Pericles Lewis

'Swift is a prodigiously talented and singular poet' – Don Share

'Swift's work is as playful as serious work gets to be'
– David Lehman

'Todd Swift is a poet besotted with language and stubbornly working out a high style of his own' – Al Alvarez

'Todd Swift is a revelation' – Terrance Hayes

'Todd Swift is the real thing' – Ilya Kaminsky

Thank you to Edwin Smet, my dear friend, a poet and artist, who designed the beautiful cover and typeset the interior. Special thanks to my beloved wife Sara; to my family, and my Bombay cat Suetonius; as well as the dedicated and cheerful team at BSPG/ Maida Vale, Amira, Cate, Jane and Nesa.